Don't Miss It

Don't Miss It
Published by Orange
a division of The reThink Group, Inc.
5870 Charlotte Lane, Suite 300
Cumming, GA 30040 U.S.A.

All Scripture quotations, unless otherwise noted, are taken from the *Holy Bible, New International Version®. NIV®.* Copyright © 1973, 1978, 1984 by International Bible Society. Used by permission of Zondervan.

Other Orange products are available online and direct from the publisher. Visit our website at www.ThinkOrange.com for more resources like these.

978-1-941259-68-9

©2016 Reggie Joiner & Kristen Ivy

Lead Editor: Mike Jeffries
Art Direction: Ryan Boon
Illustrations: Emily Carlton
Layout and Design: FiveStone

Printed in the United States of America
First Edition 2016

2 3 4 5 6 7 8 9 10 11

10/08/16

REGGIE JOINER   KRISTEN IVY

Don't Miss It

PARENT EVERY WEEK
LIKE IT COUNTS.

If you are a parent, and you want influence with your kid,
take an hour and read this book.
Then you can say you read a book today.

Or if you are in a hurry, like most parents,
at least read the left pages.
That should take about five minutes.
So you can probably finish while you're in the carpool line.

Either way, you will be reminded that you have a limited
amount of time
before your son or daughter grows up.
That's why we wrote these pages.
We just want to make sure you
don't miss it.

YOUR KIDS WILL GROW UP A LOT *FASTER* THAN YOU EVER DREAMED.

↦ DON'T MISS IT.

- -

If you are a parent with kids or teenagers, you have probably heard an older parent say something like . . .

"They grow up so fast."
"You better enjoy them while you can."
"They will be gone before you know it."

More than likely they say this because that's what someone said to them when their kids were young. So they feel like they are responsible to pass it along.

Maybe there are times you'd like to respond with . . .
"Actually, I wish they would grow up a little *faster*." Or, "No. I haven't enjoyed them at all today."
Or, "That's sad. Why can't they go somewhere *now*?"

Okay, so no parent would dare say that. Out loud at least. But what is a parent supposed to
Feel
Do
Say
when someone makes them feel like time is running out with their kids.

THE AVERAGE PARENT
HAS LESS THAN

1,000

WEEKS

FROM THE TIME THEIR KIDS ARE BORN
UNTIL THEY MOVE OUT OF THE HOUSE.

THAT CAN FEEL LIKE A LOT OF PRESSURE.

And it may seem like you could sum up most parenting advice in the following statement:

"The future of your children is coming like a freight train. You better get your act together as a parent because you're running out of time. If you're not careful, you will miss out on what's important and mess them up for the rest of their lives."

Maybe the next time someone reminds you that kids grow up fast, you should grab them by the collar, look them directly in the eye and say, *"So tell me. Exactly what are you suggesting I should do about that?"*

Okay, that may be a little too dramatic. But time is moving faster than many of us realize.

There is a clock that started ticking the day your child was born. In fact, there are less than a thousand weeks from the time a child is born until they graduate from high school.

WHEN YOU BREAK IT DOWN, IT GOES REALLY FAST.

For example, this could be the story of a typical daughter told in weeks.

Week	1	she cried all night
Week	10	she cooed and smiled
Week	40	she stood up
Week	50	she said "uh-oh"
Week	70	she flushed your keys down the potty
Week	130	she went to the potty
Week	140	she used your wall as a coloring book
Week	182	she rolled her eyes at you
Week	206	she made you a macaroni necklace
Week	234	she only answered to "Princess Jasmine"
Week	260	she began kindergarten
Week	295	she wrote a story about you
Week	315	she spoke in "Pig Latin" for two days
Week	338	she got her first visit from the Tooth Fairy
Week	364	she stopped believing in the Tooth Fairy
Week	364	she also stopped believing in Santa
Week	387	she charged you for a painted rock
Week	403	she got braces
Week	416	she had homework that confused you
Week	438	she made up a dance for the talent show
Week	459	she went to her first slumber party
Week	478	she shaved her legs
Week	494	she outgrew the kid's menu

WHAT YOU DO EVERY WEEK MATTERS.

Week 513   she beat you at Monopoly®
Week 522   she put on make-up
Week 550   she asked for a smart phone
Week 551   she begged for a smart phone
Week 572   she entered middle school
Week 573   she decided she was smarter than you
Week 597   she got her braces taken off
Week 600   she started her period
Week 624   she got a smart phone
Week 645   she decided she was a vegetarian
Week 646   she only ate hamburgers
Week 676   she legally posted on Instagram
Week 728   she attended her first high school class
Week 735   she asked when she could officially date
Week 780   she got her driver's learning permit
Week 784   she backed into the garage door
Week 806   she got her first paycheck
Week 819   she was grounded for a month
Week 820   she started unofficially dating
Week 832   she got her driver's license
Week 858   she took the SAT
Week 861   she took Harvard off her list of colleges
Week 884   she broke up with her boyfriend
Week 895   she went to her last summer camp
Week 900   she started her senior year
Week 928   she went to prom
Week 936   she graduated from high school

YOUR SON OR DAUGHTER IS SPEEDING THROUGH EACH PHASE OF LIFE FASTER AND FASTER, AND IF YOU'RE NOT CAREFUL, IT'S EASY TO MISS.

Think about it this way . . .
You will only get 365 days to know your three-year-old as a three-year-old, and then they will be four. And you will never know them again as a three-year-old.

You will only get 52 weeks to know your eight-year-old as an eight-year-old, and then they will be nine. And you will never know them again as an eight-year-old.

You will only get twelve months to know your thirteen-year-old as a thirteen-year-old, and then they will be fourteen. And you may never want to know them again as a thirteen-year-old.

So don't hurry through the present phase of your kid's life just so you can move on to whatever is next. Don't embrace an attitude that says, "*This is just a phase I need to get through as soon as possible.*" Instead, inspire your family to believe, "*This is just a phase, **and I don't want to miss it**.*"

WHAT IF YOU CREATED A
VISIBLE COUNTDOWN CLOCK
BY USING A

JAR *of* **MARBLES**

TO REPRESENT THE NUMBER OF
WEEKS YOUR SON OR DAUGHTER HAS
REMAINING AT YOUR HOUSE?

THEN YOU STARTED REMOVING

1 MARBLE EACH **WEEK?**

↦ THE FACT IS YOU HAVE A LIMITED NUMBER OF WEEKS WITH YOUR SON OR DAUGHTER.

- -

Try creating a visual countdown clock.

Start with a jar of 936 marbles. Why 936? Because that is the estimated number of weeks between birth and high school graduation.

Then reduce the number of marbles in your jar to match the actual number of weeks you have left with each child.

Then start a simple ritual:
Remove one marble every week.

Over time, the practice of losing marbles
can have a meaningful effect.

It will remind you to value your time.
It will make each week matter a little more.
It will reinforce a simple principle:

When you see how much time you have left,
you tend to do more with the time you have now.

WHEN YOU SEE
HOW MUCH TIME
YOU HAVE LEFT,

YOU TEND TO
DO MORE
WITH THE TIME YOU HAVE
NOW.

As you count down the weeks you have remaining with your child, here are some general numbers to get you started.

1	yr	884	weeks
2	yrs	832	weeks
3	yrs	780	weeks
4	yrs	728	weeks
5	yrs	676	weeks
6	yrs	624	weeks
7	yrs	572	weeks
8	yrs	520	weeks
9	yrs	468	weeks
10	yrs	416	weeks
11	yrs	364	weeks
12	yrs	312	weeks
13	yrs	260	weeks
14	yrs	208	weeks
15	yrs	156	weeks
16	yrs	104	weeks
17	yrs	52	weeks
18	yrs	0	weeks

You can make the ritual as simple or as meaningful as you like. Some families use the marble countdown as a reminder. Other parents design a weekly custom (like a meal or prayer) around removing a marble each week.

THE GOAL
IS TO
VISUALIZE TIME

IN SUCH A WAY THAT IT HELPS YOU
STAY F⊕CUSED
ON WHY

EVERY WEEK

Matters.

IF YOU'RE A PARENT,
YOU MAY BE THINKING ...

That's a really stupid idea.
I already feel enough pressure.
I can't wait to be reminded every day that I'm running out of
time with my kids.

Okay. Maybe there is a downside to creating a marble
countdown clock—like:
Depression
Guilt
Anxiety
Drinking

So, you could consider the alternative:

Ignore that time is slipping away, watch a lot of TV, and
pretend your kids will never . . .
stop eating kids' meals.
be interested in dating.
ask for the keys to your car.
grow up.

What if you could find balance between living in denial that
your kid will pack their bags and move out one day, and the
sheer panic that makes you double-bolt and padlock the doors
to keep them in?

WHAT YOU DO **EVERY WEEK** ADDS UP TO GIVE YOU **COLLECTIVE MOMENTUM** IN YOUR KID'S LIFE.

↦ VISUALIZING YOUR TIME HELPS YOU STAY FOCUSED ON THE VALUE OF YOUR RELATIONSHIP WITH YOUR KID.

It's also possible that creating a countdown clock will reprioritize how you see the time you have with your kid.

In other words, each week will matter more when you see it in the context of how many weeks you have left.

Visualizing time can help you emotionally, mentally, and practically prioritize what really matters. That's why keeping a countdown clock like a jar of marbles can make a difference.

Think about it. When you add a countdown clock to any game, competition, or exercise, it affects behavior. The next time you watch a basketball team, notice what happens to the players'
Energy
Focus
Passion
as the clock gets closer to zero.

DOES THAT MEAN YOU HAVE TO MAKE EVERY SECOND COUNT?

Or turn every minute into a teaching opportunity,
and keep a daily journal to record it all?

Nope. Not unless you want to drive yourself
and those around you crazy.

What if you just decided that you are
making history one week at a time?

The point is . . .
If you are investing in a kid or teenager,
you are already making history every week.

The problem is . . .
When you're making history,
you usually don't know it.

That's why what you're doing now matters more than it
probably feels like it does.

And that's also why this week, and every week, is really important.

Let's think about it another way.

WHILE MOST KIDS
WILL ONLY SEE
"NOW,"
YOU ARE RESPONSIBLE
TO SEE HOW THE

PAST,

PRESENT

AND

FUTURE

CONNECTS.

MOST KIDS DON'T KNOW THAT WHAT YOU'RE DOING THIS WEEK IS MAKING HISTORY.

They are kids.
They only see "now."

To them you just . . .
built a sandcastle.
took them to swim lessons.
played basketball in the driveway.
saw a movie.
ate some pizza.

But you are an adult. You see yesterday, today, and tomorrow. So, you should know better. You should realize by being present in their lives week after week in a variety of different ways, you are actually making history.

IF YOU WANT TO BUILD A
Meaningful
HISTORY
WITH YOUR KIDS,
START BY
CHANGING
WHAT HAPPENS

IT'S KIND OF LIKE A GOOD COUNTRY SONG.

Trace Adkins talks about it when he describes a dad taking his daughter fishing.

"And she thinks we're just fishin' on the riverside
Throwin' back what we couldn't fry
Drownin' worms and killin' time
Nothin' too ambitious
She ain't even thinkin' 'bout
What's really goin' on right now
But I guarantee this memory's a big 'un
And she thinks we're just fishin'"[1]

The good news is you don't have to be a . . .
gifted communicator,
famous musician,
innovative designer,
or cowboy fisherman . . .
to make meaningful history.

If you want to build a better history with your kid,
start by changing what happens this week.

1 Monty Criswell, Casey Beathard, Ed Hill. "Just Fishin'" (Nashville: Show Dog Universal Music, 2011).

WHEN WHAT YOU DO **THIS WEEK** IS REPEATED **NEXT WEEK** IT STARTS EARNING CREDIT IN A KID'S LIFE

↦ WHEN WHAT YOU DO THIS WEEK IS REPEATED NEXT WEEK, IT STARTS EARNING CREDIT IN A KID'S LIFE.

- -

Rome wasn't built in a day.

Okay, so that's a little cliché, but it's true.
Rome was built over 365,000 days.
That's what history does.

History accomplishes something over time that is . . .
unique.
powerful.
lasting.
rich.
meaningful.

Don't forget this. Some things just can't be accomplished in
a day. Or a week. They take multiple weeks. It takes time over
time to . . .
discover a vaccine.
write a novel.
play the violin.
grow a hipster beard.
raise a child.

THE BEST
WAY TO SHAPE A CHILD'S
CHARACTER + FAITH

IS THROUGH SMALL, CONSISTENT DEPOSITS.

PARENTS HAVE TO THINK LIKE AN INVESTOR WHO IS CONTRIBUTING A LITTLE EVERY WEEK.

There is no such thing as instant return on faith or character. Again, the secret is time over time.

Our attraction to immediate results can keep us so busy we never engage in work that has lasting impact. We get so preoccupied with what we can measure that we don't give attention to what we can't measure.

Did you ever stop to think:
The reason you can't monitor emotional growth is because it's too *gradual*?
The reason you can't see spiritual growth is because it's too *spiritual*?
The reason you can't predict pivotal moments is because they're too *unpredictable*?

That's why showing up again this week matters.

The best thing you can do is choose to keep . . .
investing in what you can't see.
being present for what you are not sure is happening.
trusting that your investment will ultimately see a return.

THINK ABOUT IT THIS WAY:

GOD GAVE YOU TIME WITH YOUR KIDS BECAUSE THERE ARE CERTAIN THINGS IN THEIR LIVES

THAT CAN ONLY BE ACCOMPLISHED OVER

→ → → TIME → → →

WHAT IF GOD CREATED TIME AS A CLEVER WAY TO ACCOMPLISH CERTAIN THINGS IN LIFE THAT CAN ONLY HAPPEN OVER TIME?

Maybe that's why it's important to see time in relationship to the past, present, and future. A healthy perspective of life considers all three of these tenses.

If time was created, then time obviously matters.
It has unique purpose in the greater scheme of the universe.

It's no accident the earth spins on its equator at approximately a thousand miles per hour, causing the appearance of the sun to rise and set with mathematical accuracy.

It's no accident the earth moves through space at a speed of 67,000 miles per hour causing the seasons to change in a calculated manner.

The entire universe has a predicable rhythm.

So think about the rhythm of a day, a week, a month, and even a year in the life of your family.

Create A Rhythm

IN YOUR HOME
THAT LEVERAGES

 ROUTINE TIMES
TO INFLUENCE YOUR CHILD
EVERY WEEK.

UNDERSTANDING HOW TO LEVERAGE THE NATURAL RHYTHMS IN LIFE CAN GIVE YOU MORE INFLUENCE IN A KID'S LIFE.

The cosmos works together like gears on a clock.
If we study it, we can evaluate and predict how things . . .
grow.
change.
age.

It seems obvious that time exists for a purpose.

The most significant gift we can give a kid is what we give them over time. That makes what you do this week and next week and the week after that strategic. As a parent, it's important to realize there are certain things that can only be . . .
communicated,
understood,
and discovered over time.

IF YOU WANT YOUR CHILD
TO GROW UP WITH A HEALTHY SENSE OF

WORTH

DIRECTION

PERSPECTIVE

BELONGING

SIGNIFICANCE

CONNECTION

... THEN YOU NEED TO BE
INTENTIONAL ABOUT WHAT YOU
DO OVER TIME.

↦ THE FUTURE OF CHILDREN IS BUILT ON WHAT YOU GIVE THEM OVER TIME.

— —

. . . Kids don't experience worth because they are shown affection once, but by unconditional LOVE over time.

. . . Kids are not motivated to change their lifestyle by one phrase, but when they hear consistent WORDS over time.

. . . Kids don't understand the world through a single event, but through a collection of STORIES over time.

. . . Kids don't know they belong because of a special invitation, but by feeling welcomed in a TRIBE over time.

. . . Kids don't find significance through accomplishing a task, but by doing meaningful WORK over time.

. . . Kids don't discover how to enjoy life because of one thrilling moment, but by experiencing joy and FUN over time.

YOU NEED TO MAKE SURE YOU

DON'T MISS

THIS **PHASE** OF THEIR LIFE SO

THEY WON'T MISS SOME THINGS
THEY NEED TO KNOW + EXPERIENCE.

YOU CAN'T REWIND YOUR KID'S LIFE.

You can't stop the clock from ticking. But here are a few things you *can* do as a parent:

You *can* pause at significant moments and celebrate what is happening while it is still happening.

You *can* understand who they are now
so you can shape who they will become later.

You *can* leverage this present phase
so you can impact their future potential.

If you don't miss this phase, then maybe your kid won't miss something they will need for their future.

So keep reading, and remember this principle:
**If you don't miss out on your kid's life,
then maybe your kid won't miss out**
on some important things about life.

HERE'S A **TOUGH** QUESTION:

HOW WOULD YOUR **KIDS**

GRADE YOU ON HOW WELL YOU KNOW THEM

RIGHT NOW?

WHAT IF YOUR SON OR DAUGHTER GAVE YOU A POP QUIZ WITH QUESTIONS LIKE . . .

Who is my favorite actor?
What is my favorite food?
Who is my best friend?

Okay, those may be easy, but what about . . .
Who was I talking to online last night?
What scares me the most?
Why were my feelings hurt today?

What grade do you think your son or daughter would give you if they graded you on how well you know them?

The problem is most of us usually don't know our kids as well as we think we do. It's so easy to miss what is really going on.

Don't ever buy into this myth:
If I am present, I will know what I need to know.

As important as it is to show up, you can be where you should be and still miss what is right in front of you. That happens for a number of reasons.

SOMETIMES YOU MISS IT BECAUSE
YOU DONT REMEMBER
WHAT **YOU DONT REMEMBER.**

ADULTS TEND TO FORGET
THAT *Every Kid* IS

MADE IN THE IMAGE OF GOD.

You sometimes miss it because
YOU DON'T REMEMBER WHAT YOU DON'T REMEMBER.

Be honest. Sometimes it's just easy to forget what you need to remember.

Maybe it's because . . .
you get busy doing what you do.
you get hyper-focused on fixing a problem.
you get super-analytical about a spiritual issue.

But what would happen if every parent could remember a single profound truth about every kid?
Regardless of their attitude,
regardless of their tone,
regardless of their frustration,
what if every parent simply remembered:
Every kid is made in the image of God.

Okay. Maybe you already knew that. But you have to admit it's easy to forget. Sure, when your child was first born, it was easy to think, *I can see the image of God in this baby.* Then after a few sleepless nights and endless pooping, you became a little skeptical.

THAT MEANS YOUR SON OR DAUGHTER
HAS THE DIVINE CAPACITY...

TO *Believe, Imagine & Love.*

TO CARE, RELATE, + TRUST.

TO REASON, IMPROVE, AND LEAD

THAT'S **A LOT** OF POTENTIAL.

It should be obvious though, right?
Humans are very different from animals.
Lions don't imagine God.
Tigers don't try to improve their character.
Bears don't reason about life after death.
But people do. And in case you haven't noticed,
kids are people too.

Stop for a moment and think about it. If every kid is created in
the image of God, then every kid has a divine capacity . . .
to believe, imagine, and love.
to care, relate, and trust.
to reason, improve, and lead.
That's a lot of potential.

You may be thinking, *I'm not sure my kid reflects God's image,
although they do make me talk to God a lot.*
You may wonder how they can possibly reflect God's
image when . . .
your toddler is throwing a tantrum
           because you said, "You can't eat dirt."
your kid is eating a candy bar
           he stole from his big sister.
your teenager is wearing an outfit
           she snuck to school in her backpack.

SOME OF US HAVE BEEN SO PROGRAMMED TO SEE WHAT IS WRONG ABOUT OUR KIDS THAT WE HAVE FORGOTTEN HOW TO SEE WHAT IS RIGHT ABOUT THEM.

YOUR KID IS ALSO A REFLECTION OF YOUR IMAGE, TOO.

Yep. Just like *you* have a dark side, so does your kid. That's why they embarrass you sometimes, right?

Some people call it "sin nature." It's been around for a while. Actually, it's been here since the beginning of time. It showed up when the first guy (who was also made in the image of God) made a choice that messed up the image of God for the rest of us. And then it was handed down to you and then to your kid.

But most parents don't have to be reminded that their kids have a dark side. Have you ever noticed how easy it is for a parent to see what's wrong about their kids and how easy it is to miss what is right?

That's why you need to look closer—and pay attention—so you can still see the flicker of God's image in your own child. Some adults miss it because they treat kids like they are not old enough, smart enough, mature enough, important enough, or even spiritual enough to really do anything significant. But these grown-ups aren't remembering what they need to remember.

WHEN YOU REMIND YOURSELF
consistently

THAT YOUR KIDS ARE
MADE IN THE
IMAGE of
GOD,

IT CAN CHANGE:

HOW YOU **SEE** THEM.

HOW THEY SEE THEMSELVES.

AND EVEN HOW THEY SEE GOD.

DO YOU GET IT?

Every kid has the God-given potential to do amazing things . . .
the three-year-old who knows every word of every song
in *Frozen*,
the first grader who knows how to build a Star Destroyer
out of LEGOs,
the third grader who knows how to spell "interlocutory" at
a spelling bee,
the seventh grader who knows how to navigate technology
like he invented it.

Why?
Because every kid is created in the image of God.

You should never underestimate your kid's potential to learn,
grow, build, innovate, and simply do something good because
they have the ability to reflect their Creator.

**When you learn to see God's image in your kid, it increases
the potential for your kid to see God.** And when kids begin
to understand they are made in the image of God, they tend
to look at the world and themselves differently.

WHEN KIDS START BELIEVING THEY ARE **MADE** IN THE **IMAGE** OF **GOD**, IT CAN IMPACT HOW THEY...

☑ MAKE DECISIONS

USE TECHNOLOGY

♡ ♡ VIEW SEX

TREAT THEIR BODY

— AND —

CARE ABOUT PEOPLE

This one perspective can affect how they . . .
make decisions,
view sex,
use technology,
relate to parents,
see the church,
care about people,
and trust God.

Don't make the mistake of missing it.
You wouldn't just be ignoring a child.
You could also be ignoring God.
And you definitely would be ignoring the potential
every kid has to experience God.

Maybe that's why Jesus was so emphatic one day with His
disciples. Jesus knew they needed to remember what they
weren't remembering. So He placed a child in front of them
and He firmly reminded them, *"Whoever welcomes one such
child in my name welcomes me . . ."*

It's kind of like Jesus was saying, "I want you to treat your
kids like you would treat Me, and I am *God*. So just make
sure you understand when you welcome kids, it's like you are
welcoming God."
Jesus made kids a pretty big deal.

BY THE WAY,
HAVE YOU EVER WONDERED
WHAT MAKES YOU **LOVE** YOUR KIDS
SO MUCH?

YOU ARE MADE IN THE IMAGE
OF GOD, TOO.

IT'S THE NATURE OF A HEAVENLY
FATHER FLICKERING IN YOU
THAT MAKES YOU WANT TO BE A
BETTER PARENT.

PARENTS ARE PEOPLE, TOO.

That means you are also made in the image of God.

Think about it this way:
You were created in the image of a heavenly Father.

Have you ever wondered what makes you want to be a better parent? Have you ever been amazed by how much you love your kids? It's the image of your heavenly Father flickering in you as a mom or dad.

That's why every parent shares one thing
in common when it comes to their kids.

Every parent wants their son or daughter to
have the best future they can possibly have.

You don't just want your kids to
be happy, or successful, or famous.
You want them to live the fullest life possible.
You want them to experience unconditional love.
You want them to know they matter.

Why? Because you are a parent created in the image of a heavenly Father who loves them too.

ANOTHER REASON YOU MISS
→ WHAT'S HAPPENING ←
IN YOUR KID'S LIFE IS BECAUSE

YOU DON'T SEE,
WHAT DON'T
YOU SEE

Another reason you miss it is because
YOU DON'T SEE WHAT YOU DON'T SEE.

Imagine for a minute that every kid has an invisible sign with an invisible question they need someone to help them answer at each phase of life. Why? Because each phase has a unique set of issues a child has to learn how to navigate.

For example . . .
Toddlers have constantly changing abilities.
Second graders begin to compare and form groups.
Sixth graders are navigating puberty.
Tenth graders want a new level of freedom.

That's why it's so important for parents to learn to see what is going on at each phase of a kid's life.

Most kids never ask their invisible questions out loud. So it's up to you as a parent to discern a child's hidden questions and respond. That's what makes parenting a little complicated. You have to learn to see what can't be seen so you can be what your kid needs you to be.

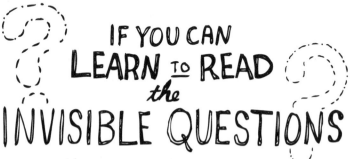

IF YOU CAN **LEARN TO READ** *the* INVISIBLE QUESTIONS YOUR KIDS ARE ASKING AT EVERY PHASE, YOU WILL HAVE A DIFFERENT KIND OF INFLUENCE ON THEIR FUTURE

THE BETTER YOU KNOW YOUR KIDS, THE BETTER YOU WILL BE ABLE TO LEAD THEM.

But here's a problem. Your kids keep changing, which means their issues keep changing.

Your kids are navigating an important journey from childhood to adulthood. So remember:
You are not raising children.
You are raising adults.

As a parent, you have to resist the temptation to fix your child's problems and learn instead to respond in a way that helps them grow. It starts with understanding how to stay alert to what is actually happening at every phase and learning how to read the signs.

Since every phase of a kid's life has unique challenges, you should become aware of the kind of questions that are asked at each phase.

Preschoolers tend to ask "AM I" questions.
Am I safe?
Am I okay?
Am I able?

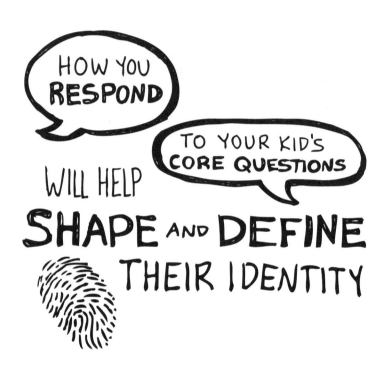

Elementary-age kids tend to ask "DO I" questions.
Do I have your attention?
Do I have what it takes?
Do I have any friends?

As they move toward middle school, there is a shift in the nature of a child's questions. They become more philosophical and relational.

Middle school students tend to ask questions like . . .
Who do I like?
Who am I?
Where do I belong?

During high school, the questions continue to shift from concrete to abstract, from black and white to various shades of gray.
Why should I believe?
How can I matter?
What will I do?

At the center of each question is the pronoun "I." That's because each of these questions reflects a part of a child's developing identity. How you respond to these questions can shape who your son or daughter becomes. So don't miss it.

THERE MAY ALSO BE TIMES
YOU MISS IT BECAUSE
You don't
ANTICIPATE
WHAT YOU DON'T
Anticipate.

There may also be times you miss it because
YOU DON'T ANTICIPATE
WHAT YOU DON'T ANTICIPATE.

Parenting humans can be unpredictable. Every kid is different and there are no formulas. It's hard to anticipate everything. So in a sense, you should anticipate not anticipating a few things.

But there is another list of things that are very predictable— that is, if you take the time to think ahead about what's coming in the typical kid's life.

Consider this fact:
Over 100 billion people have lived and died on planet Earth.

That's 100 billion history lessons to teach us what typically happens in someone's life as they grow up.

So after watching 100 billion people live and die, experts are smart enough to know there are patterns that can be anticipated in the average kid's life.

Even though there will be surprises, there are a number of things that should never surprise you.

ANTICIPATING

SIMPLY MEANS YOU

AT WHAT WILL PROBABLY HAPPEN AND GET READY FOR IT.

If you take some time, reflect on your own life and do a little homework as a parent, you can anticipate what you *should* anticipate.

There are some pretty obvious moments
when you should never say,
"I didn't see that coming."

For example, don't be surprised when your . . .
baby spits up.
toddler wets his pants.
five-year-old starts school.
first grader loses a tooth.
fourth grader asks for a smart phone.
sixth grader eats a whole pizza.
ninth grade son's voice changes.
eleventh grader asks for your car keys.
senior graduates and moves out after living with you for less than a thousand weeks.

So you might as well put one thousand marbles in a jar and start the countdown. That way you will have a visual reminder that there are some predictable issues that will affect your kid at every phase.

AS A PARENT,
YOU NEED TO LEARN TO
PREDICT &
REDEFINE
HOW YOU PARENT
AT EVERY PHASE.

The challenge is to think ahead so you have a plan.
You will need to get a car seat.
You will need to go to the doctor for vaccinations.
You will need to enroll your child in elementary school.
You will need to save for college.
You will need to start an ongoing conversation about sex.
You will need to establish boundaries for dating.
You will need to sign up for the PTA.
You will need to screen friends.
You will need to manage technology.
You may even need a few therapy sessions.

But with every phase, no matter how well you think you
know your child, the changes will force you to relearn some
parenting skills.

Parenting a preschooler takes different skills than parenting a
middle schooler. (Although there are awkward conversations
about body parts in both.)

Convincing a two-year-old takes different skills than
influencing a tenth grader. (Although you will sense a battle
for independence in both.)

So anticipate what is coming before it gets here and learn to
frequently redefine your life as a parent.

THE IMPORTANT QUESTION
YOU NEED TO ASK AS A PARENT IS:

DO YOU HAVE A

STRATEGY

TO DEVELOP YOUR KIDS

☑ EMOTIONALLY

☑ RELATIONALLY

AND EVEN

☑ SPIRITUALLY?

AT LEAST ANTICIPATE THE FUTURE ENOUGH TO START ASKING YOURSELF THIS QUESTION:

What is the strategy for the relational, emotional, moral, and even spiritual development of my kid?

It may seem like a daunting question at first. But if you want to do everything possible to protect the future of your children, then you need to parent like your child's emotional intelligence is as important to your kid's future as physical health or education.

Admit it. You have a strategy for other parts of their life. You take them to school. You take them to dance lessons. You take them to the doctor. You take them to baseball practice.

Most parents will admit they need a better strategy for the emotional and spiritual development of their kids. But those same parents are still paralyzed when it comes to knowing exactly what to do.

So if you don't want to miss it, what should you do about it? Keep reading for three things that can get you started:

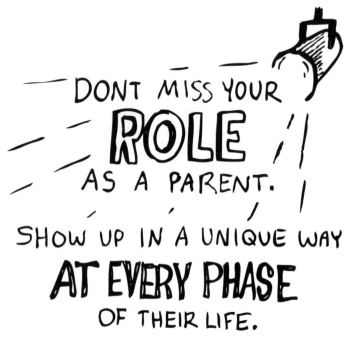

DONT MISS YOUR **ROLE** AS A PARENT.

SHOW UP IN A UNIQUE WAY **AT EVERY PHASE** OF THEIR LIFE.

  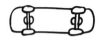

① DON'T MISS YOUR ROLE

No one has the potential to influence your son or daughter like you. Yep. That's a lot of pressure. And it can be confusing. You are a mix of teacher, coach, counselor, and friend. So here's a one-sentence job description to keep you focused.

If you have a preschooler,
EMBRACE their physical needs.
Spend the first 200 weeks helping your child develop a sense of security and confidence.

If you have an elementary-age child,
ENGAGE their interests.
Appeal to your child's curiosity to broaden their knowledge and abilities.

If you have a middle schooler,
AFFIRM their personal journey.
Show up consistently to give your kid stability as they navigate changes and discover their potential.

If you have a high schooler,
MOBILIZE their potential.
Guide your teenager's values and passions as they launch into the new realities of an adult world.

DON'T MISS

THIS WEEK

IN YOUR KID'S LIFE.

Leverage YOUR ROUTINE

FAMILY TIMES TOGETHER

TO SHAPE YOUR KID'S FUTURE

2 DON'T MISS THIS WEEK

When you count how many weeks you have, you will tend to make your weeks count. So know the number of weeks for each one of your kids. Count how many you have left with each of them. Then create a weekly rhythm for your family to be intentional about shaping their future. You can actually establish a few routines in your home to help you invest in how your kids are growing emotionally, socially, and spiritually.

When you share a MEAL TIME, you can establish values with intentional conversations while you eat.

When you pause at BED TIME, you strengthen your relationship through heart conversations.

When you leverage DRIVE TIME, you can interpret life during informal conversations as you travel.

When you connect positively in the MORNING TIME, you can instill purpose and give fuel for their day.

So take your CUE every week to make your time together with your kids count.

DON'T MISS
SUNDAY.

CONNECT YOUR KIDS TO OTHER
CARING ADULTS WHO WILL
TREAT THEM LIKE THEY
ARE MADE IN

THE IMAGE OF GOD.

3 DON'T MISS SUNDAY

As a parent, you are not the only adult influence your child needs. Sooner or later, a shift will happen in your relationship with your son or daughter. When it happens, it may seem like they will care more about what other adults say than what you say. Don't take it personally. Leverage this shift to "widen the circle" of positive influences in your child's life.

That's why a church or faith community should play such a significant role in your family. You're probably thinking, *Yep, I was wondering when this book was going to bring up church.* But consider the obvious. A church has the potential to connect your son or daughter to a caring leader who believes in their future like you do. How many other places do you know that connect kids to a leader who gives them a safe place to talk about God and life?

Every kid is looking for a tribe outside their family where they can find a place to belong. Either they will find somewhere on their own, or you can help them find a place that reflects your values and heart for their future. So why not connect them to other adults who will also treat them like they are made in the image of God?

THIS BOOK WAS
⬇ SHORT ⬇

BECAUSE THE PHASES ARE, TOO.
WHEN LIFE GETS BUSY—**AND IT WILL**—
REMEMBER THESE SIMPLE TRUTHS:

WHAT YOU DO AS A PARENT EVERY WEEK MATTERS.

WHEN YOU COUNT YOUR WEEKS,
YOU TEND TO MAKE YOUR
WEEKS COUNT.

IF YOU WANT TO INFLUENCE
YOUR CHILD'S FUTURE, GET TO
KNOW WHO THEY ARE TODAY.

THE CLOCK IS TICKING. TIME KEEPS
MOVING. BUT YOU GET THE CHOICE TO
MAKE HISTORY AS A FAMILY
EVERY WEEK.

IT'S JUST A PHASE, DON'T MISS IT.